THE BEST MLB
HITTERS
OF ALL TIME

By Will Graves

Published by ABDO Publishing Company, PO Box 398166, Minneapolis, MN 55439. Copyright © 2014 by Abdo Consulting Group, Inc. International copyrights reserved in all countries. No part of this book may be reproduced in any form without written permission from the publisher. SportsZone™ is a trademark and logo of ABDO Publishing Company.

Printed in the United States of America,
North Mankato, Minnesota
092013
012014

Editor: Chrös McDougall
Series Designer: Christa Schneider

Photo credits: AP Images, cover (left), 1 (left), 9, 11, 15, 17, 19, 21, 23, 27, 31, 33, 35, 37, 39, 41, 43, 45, 47, 49, 51; Kevin Terrell/AP Images, cover (right), 1 (right); National Baseball Library, Cooperstown, N.Y./ AP Images, 7; Tigers Archives/AP Images, 13; Bill Chaplis/AP Images, 25; Warren M. Winterbottom/AP Images, 29; Mark Avery/AP Images, 53; Daniel Gluskoter/Icon SMI, 55; Oakland Tribune/Icon SMI, 57; Jeff Moffett/Icon SMI, 59; Eric Gay/AP Images, 61

Library of Congress Control Number: 2013945899

Cataloging-in-Publication Data
Graves, Will.
 The best MLB hitters of all time / Will Graves.
   p. cm. -- (Major League Baseball's best ever)
Includes bibliographical references and index.
ISBN 978-1-62403-114-4
1. Major League Baseball (Organization)--Juvenile literature. 2. Batting (Baseball)--Juvenile literature. 3. Batters (Baseball)--Juvenile literature. I. Title.
796.357--dc23

                                    2013945899

TABLE OF CONTENTS

INTRODUCTION

Thwack! **The sound of a baseball hitting a wooden bat is as old as the game itself.**

Not all thwacks are created equal, though. Some Major League Baseball (MLB) sluggers crush the ball over the outfield wall for home runs. Others thrive on small ball. They can connect with just about any pitch and put it into play for a single or a double. And the greatest hitters in American League (AL) and National League (NL) history could do both. They hit for power and for average, getting on base, driving in runs, and helping their teams win games.

Here are some of the best hitters in MLB history.

BABE RUTH

The legend of George Herman "Babe" Ruth was well known to baseball fans by 1932. Ruth had begun his career in 1914 as a standout pitcher for the Boston Red Sox. The Red Sox, however, sold him to the New York Yankees in 1920. And in New York, he became a full-time outfielder and the greatest home-run hitter of his era. He had already led the team to three World Series titles.

Ruth was still the biggest star on baseball's best team in 1932. And his Yankees were heavy favorites to beat the Chicago Cubs for another World Series title. But Ruth was older at age 37. Some Cubs players and fans mocked the aging star.

Ruth made them pay.

Babe Ruth became baseball's greatest home run hitter of his era after joining the New York Yankees in 1920.

Game 3 was tied 4–4 in the fifth inning. Ruth stepped to the plate and pointed his bat. Some say he pointed it at the Chicago players. Others say he pointed it at Chicago's pitcher. The legend says he pointed the bat beyond the center field wall, where he intended to hit the ball. And that is where it went. The Yankees won the game and the World Series. Ruth's "called shot" went down in history.

He was certainly famous without it, though. Ruth was a slugging machine at a time when home runs were rare. The single-season home run record was 27 when Ruth's career began. He bettered that 14 times. His best season was 1927, when he hit 60. In total, Ruth hit an amazing 714 home runs. Plus he helped his teams win seven World Series titles in his 22 seasons. It is no wonder "The Bambino" went down as baseball's iconic player.

12

The number of times Ruth led the AL in home runs. No other player through 2013 has led either the AL or the NL in home runs more than seven times in his career.

Babe Ruth remains one of the most beloved baseball players of all time.

BABE RUTH

Positions: Pitcher and Outfielder

Hometown: Baltimore, Maryland

Height, Weight: 6 feet 2, 215 pounds

Birth Date: February 6, 1895

Teams: Boston Red Sox (1914–19)
   New York Yankees (1920–34)
   Boston Braves (1935)

All-Star Games: 1933, 1934

MVP Award: 1923

TY COBB

Ty Cobb earned the nickname "Georgia Peach" from the state in which he grew up. Yet there was nothing fuzzy or sweet about the way he played baseball.

Cobb was the most feared hitter of his time. He spent 24 seasons dominating the game and scaring opponents with his fierce will to win.

Cobb liked to say he played with a "fire in his belly." And he did not mind if that fire rubbed others the wrong way. For more than two decades, Cobb's competitiveness helped make him one of the most dangerous hitters to ever put on a uniform.

Ty Cobb of the Detroit Tigers warms up before a 1922 game.

Cobb played with a mix of speed and power. He was like a scientist at the plate. He would pick an area of the field where he wanted to send the ball. Then he would adjust his swing and send the ball in that direction. Cobb only hit 117 home runs in his career. But he finished with an amazing 4,191 hits. His career batting average was .367. It remained the best through 2013.

Cobb was not done when he reached base either. He stole 892 bases during his career, often sliding feet first with his spikes up.

The outfielder's approach did not win him many friends. But he did not care as long as it helped his team win the game. Cobb helped the Detroit Tigers make the World Series three times, but they lost each one. He retired in 1928 and was inducted into the Baseball Hall of Fame as part of the first class in 1936.

9

The number of consecutive years in which Cobb led the AL in batting (1907 to 1915)—the longest streak by any player in baseball history.

Ty Cobb was one of the greatest base stealers in MLB history.

TY COBB

Position: Center Fielder

Hometown: Narrows, Georgia

Height, Weight: 6 feet 1, 175 pounds

Birth Date: December 18, 1886

Teams: Detroit Tigers (1905–26)
   Philadelphia Athletics (1927–28)

MVP Award: 1911

LOU GEHRIG

Lou Gehrig stepped up to the microphone on July 4, 1939. It was "Lou Gehrig Day" at Yankee Stadium. His voice quivered as he spoke. The great first baseman had been forced to retire earlier that season. A mysterious disease had begun to affect his muscles. Nevertheless, Gehrig told the crowd that day that he was the "luckiest man on the face of the earth." Yankee fans might have disagreed. For 14 seasons, they had been lucky to have Gehrig in their lineup.

Yankees outfielder Babe Ruth was a baseball icon. Gehrig batted right behind him in the order. Together they gave the Yankees the best one-two punch in baseball history.

Although sometimes overshadowed by New York Yankees teammate Babe Ruth, Lou Gehrig was an all-time great hitter.

Ruth was the charismatic star. Gehrig was known for simply coming to the ballpark and almost always playing very well. In fact, Gehrig did not miss one game between June 1, 1925, and April 30, 1939. And he was incredibly consistent during that time. He could hit for both power and average. Fans called him "The Iron Horse" because he was so strong and so steady.

Gehrig put up career numbers that nearly matched Ruth's. He hit 493 career home runs, drove in 1,992 runs, and batted .340 for his career. He twice led the AL in home runs. And he led the league in runs batted in (RBIs) five times.

Gehrig was just 35 years old when he noticed his body was starting to break down. Less than two years after his famous speech at Yankee Stadium, he passed away from the disease they now call "Lou Gehrig's Disease."

.361

Gehrig's batting average in 34 World Series games. He helped lead the Yankees to six championships in seven World Series appearances during his career.

Yankees first baseman Lou Gehrig crosses home plate for a run during Game 1 of the 1938 World Series.

LOU GEHRIG

Position: First Baseman

Hometown: New York, New York

Height, Weight: 6 feet, 200 pounds

Birth Date: June 19, 1903

Team: New York Yankees (1923–39)

All-Star Games: 1933, 1934, 1935, 1936, 1937, 1938, 1939

MVP Awards: 1927, 1936

JOE DIMAGGIO

It was May 15, 1941. The usually powerful New York Yankees were off to a slow start. Center fielder Joe DiMaggio stepped into the batter's box hoping to give his team a spark.

"The Yankee Clipper" got one hit that day. Then he got two more the next day. In every game for two months, DiMaggio managed at least one hit. His 56-game hitting streak became the talk of the nation. It set a record that had yet to be broken through 2013. More importantly to DiMaggio, it helped the Yankees start winning.

New York was just 14–14 when DiMaggio's streak started. When it finished, they were in first place. They went on to win the AL pennant and the World Series.

The New York Yankees' Joe DiMaggio singles to extend his hitting streak to 42 games on June 29, 1941.

DiMaggio led New York to the World Series 10 times in his 13-year career. The Yankees won all but one of those Fall Classics.

DiMaggio retired in 1951 with 2,214 career hits and 361 career home runs. His numbers could have been even better. However, the United States entered World War II in 1941. And DiMaggio missed the 1943, 1944, and 1945 seasons while serving in the Army. He traveled around the world playing in games to entertain the US troops.

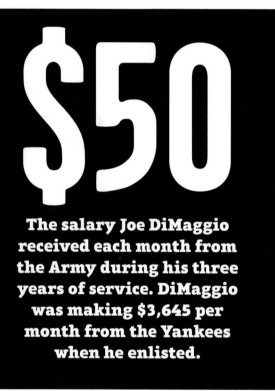

$50

The salary Joe DiMaggio received each month from the Army during his three years of service. DiMaggio was making $3,645 per month from the Yankees when he enlisted.

"Jolting Joe" hardly missed a beat when he returned to the Yankees in 1946. He won his third Most Valuable Player (MVP) Award in 1947. And he led the AL in home runs and RBIs in 1948.

However, he is best remembered for his hitting streak in the summer of 1941.

Joe DiMaggio hits a solo home run against the New York Giants during Game 5 of the 1937 World Series.

JOE DIMAGGIO

Position: Center Fielder

Hometown: Martinez, California

Height, Weight: 6 feet 2, 193 pounds

Birth Date: November 25, 1914

Team: New York Yankees (1936–42, 1946–51)*

All-Star Games: 1936, 1937, 1938, 1939, 1940, 1941, 1942, 1946, 1947, 1948, 1949, 1950, 1951

MVP Awards: 1939, 1941, 1947

*Did not play 1943–45 because of military service

TED WILLIAMS

Outfielder Ted Williams could have taken the day off. It was the final day of the 1941 season. The Boston Red Sox had a doubleheader against the Philadelphia Athletics. And Williams had a .400 batting average.

Red Sox manager Joe Cronin said Williams could sit out. That would ensure that Williams achieved the batting average milestone. But Williams had no interest in taking the easy way out. Instead, he played both games and went 6-for-9. His final average was .406. No player has hit .400 for a season since.

"Teddy Ballgame" loved hitting. He often talked to other players about it. He even wrote a book called *The Science of Hitting*. The left-handed Williams also had great talent and a perfect swing. He collected 2,654 hits during 19 major league seasons.

Boston Red Sox left fielder Ted Williams was known for his near-perfect swing.

Williams's career was interrupted twice by war. He enlisted in the Marines during World War II. Later, he was called to the Korean War. He served as a fighter pilot. Williams flew 39 missions for the Marines before leaving and returning to baseball. And he was still a star.

Williams led the majors with a .388 batting average as a 38-year-old in 1957. He then retired with style after the 1960 season. Williams hit a home run in his final at-bat. However, Williams famously refused to tip his cap to the fans after the home run. He had vowed to never again do that after home fans booed him early in his career. Nonetheless, he hoped the Fenway Park faithful would have good memories of him.

"All I want out of life is that when I walk down the street folks will say, 'There goes the greatest hitter that ever lived,'" Williams said.

2

The number of times Williams won baseball's Triple Crown. He led the AL in batting average, home runs, and RBIs in 1942 and 1947.

A crowd gathers to watch the Red Sox's Ted Williams take batting practice at spring training in 1950.

TED WILLIAMS

Position: Left Fielder

Hometown: San Diego, California

Height, Weight: 6 feet 3, 205 pounds

Birth Date: August 30, 1918

Team: Boston Red Sox (1939–42, 1946–60)*

All-Star Games:1940, 1941, 1942, 1946, 1947, 1948, 1949, 1950, 1951, 1953, 1954, 1955, 1956, 1957, 1958, 1959, 1960

MVP Awards: 1946, 1949

*Did not play in 1943–45 because of military service

STAN MUSIAL

The St. Louis Cardinals signed Stan Musial in 1938 to be a pitcher. However, that dream died when he injured his shoulder in the minor leagues. Instead, Musial moved to the outfield and became one of the most consistent hitters of all time.

Musial became the face of the Cardinals during his 22 seasons. He was a fixture first in the outfield and later at first base. But his true home always seemed to be the batter's box. Musial was of average size at 6 feet tall and 175 pounds. Yet he cast a huge shadow whenever he stepped to the plate. He could hit for power, collecting 475 home runs during his career. He was fast, too. Musial led the NL in doubles eight times and in triples five times.

Stan Musial was beloved in St. Louis not just for his great hitting but also for his outgoing personality.

His real talent, though, was knowing when to swing. Musial rarely struck out. And it was that gift that turned him into an All-Star year after year.

The Cardinals won three World Series during Musial's playing days. Most consider him to be the greatest player in team history. But just as important as his play on the field was his grace off of it. Musial was humble and always nice to the fans. He was awarded the Medal of Freedom in 2010 by President Barack Obama for his service to the game.

"All he was was incredibly good for an incredibly long time and an unbelievably nice guy," said Bob Costas, an award-winning sportscaster whose career began in St. Louis.

5

The number of home runs Musial hit in a doubleheader on May 2, 1954, against the New York Giants—a record that still stood in 2013.

St. Louis Cardinals star Stan Musial hits against the Philadelphia Phillies during a 1946 game.

STAN MUSIAL

Positions: Outfielder and First Baseman

Hometown: Donora, Pennsylvania

Height, Weight: 6 feet, 175 pounds

Birth Date: November 21, 1920

Team: St. Louis Cardinals (1941–44, 1946–63)*

All-Star Games: 1943, 1944, 1946, 1947, 1948, 1949, 1950, 1951, 1952, 1953, 1954, 1955, 1956, 1957, 1958, 1959, 1960, 1961, 1962, 1963

MVP Awards: 1943, 1946, 1948

*Did not play in 1945 because of military service

MICKEY MANTLE

Mickey Mantle learned to hit as a boy growing up in Oklahoma. Every day he would hit tennis balls against an old tin shed. Mantle's father, Mutt, would pitch right-handed while Mantle hit left-handed. Then Mantle's grandfather, Charlie, would pitch left-handed while Mantle hit right-handed.

The goal was to make Mantle a dangerous hitter from both sides of home plate. And it worked. Mantle became known as the greatest switch-hitter during his 18 seasons with the New York Yankees. His 536 career home runs are the most by a switch-hitter in baseball history through 2013. In 1953, Mantle hit a home run that traveled 565 feet (172 m). That was the longest home run ever recorded.

New York Yankees outfielder Mickey Mantle was one of baseball's all-time great switch hitters.

Mantle wasn't just a slugger, though. He also was one of the best outfielders of his generation. He had a strong arm and plenty of speed to track down fly balls.

Amazingly, Mantle played his entire major league career with an injury. As a rookie in 1951, Mantle tried to avoid fellow outfielder Joe DiMaggio. Mantle ended up injuring his right knee on the play. He was forced to tightly wrap his leg before every game for the rest of his career. But it did not limit his ability.

Led by Mantle, the Yankees were a powerhouse in the 1950s and early 1960s. New York won seven World Series titles with Mantle in the lineup. He was inducted into the Hall of Fame in 1974. It was the end of a long journey from the old tin shed where Mantle had practiced the swing that made him a superstar.

18

The number of home runs Mantle hit in the World Series—the most of any player in baseball history through 2013.

The Yankees' Mickey Mantle swings at a pitch in 1967 during his then-record-tying 2,164th career game as a Yankee.

MICKEY MANTLE

Positions: Center Fielder and First Baseman

Hometown: Spavinaw, Oklahoma

Height, Weight: 5 feet 11, 195 pounds

Birth Date: October 20, 1931

Team: New York Yankees (1951–68)

All-Star Games: 1952, 1953, 1954, 1955, 1956, 1957, 1958, 1959, 1960, 1961, 1962, 1963, 1964, 1965, 1966, 1967, 1968

Gold Glove: 1962

MVP Awards: 1956, 1957, 1962

WILLIE MAYS

Willie Mays spent nearly two decades as one of baseball's most feared hitters. Yet the biggest play of his career might have been in the outfield. The speedy center fielder was playing for the New York Giants in the 1954 World Series. In Game 1, the Giants and the Cleveland Indians were tied in the eighth inning. But the Indians had two men on base.

Vic Wertz then hit a long fly ball to center. The ball flew over Mays's head. It looked like a sure hit. But Mays somehow tracked it down. He caught the ball at full speed just in front of the wall with his back to the plate. The Giants went on to win the game and the World Series.

Willie Mays is known as one of the best all-around baseball players of all time.

"The Catch" is one of the most famous plays in baseball history.
It also sent a message that "The Say Hey Kid" was ready to take over the game. During his remarkable 22 years in the major leagues, Mays became one of the best players to ever suit up.

He hit 660 home runs during his career. That was the fourth-highest total through 2013. He also twice won the NL MVP Award. And he was awarded 12 Gold Gloves for his great work in the outfield.

Mays tied a record by appearing in 24 All-Star Games. Ted Williams, the great hitter for the Boston Red Sox, once said "they invented the All-Star Game for Willie Mays." Maybe that is because, in a way, Mays turned every game into the All-Star Game. Whether it was his monster home runs or his incredible catches, Mays always seemed to put on a show.

4

The number of times Mays led the NL in steals—proof that he was not just strong, but plenty fast, too.

36

The New York Giants' Willie Mays slides home during a 1952 game against the Philadelphia Phillies.

WILLIE MAYS

Position: Center Fielder

Hometown: Westfield, Alabama

Height, Weight: 5 feet 10, 170 pounds

Birth Date: May 6, 1931

Teams: New York/San Francisco
Giants (1951–52, 1954–72)*
New York Mets (1972–73)

All-Star Games: 1954–73

Gold Gloves: 1957–68

MVP Awards: 1954, 1965

Rookie of the Year: 1951

*Did not play in 1953 because of military
service

HANK AARON

Hank Aaron stepped into the batter's box, dug his feet into the dirt, and prepared to do the unthinkable. For decades, Babe Ruth's record of 714 home runs was thought to be unbreakable. Yet Aaron slowly closed in on Ruth. People around the nation followed with great interest. Aaron tied the mark with a home run on April 4, 1974. Four days later, he sent a long, fly ball behind the left field wall. It was his 715th home run.

Aaron finished his career with 755 home runs. However, it was that 715th that lives on as one of the most famous moments in baseball history.

Atlanta Braves outfielder Hank Aaron smiles at a press conference in 1974 after hitting his 715th career home run.

Aaron was usually reserved. He did not seek attention like other star players of his time. And he rarely dominated. Aaron never hit more than 47 home runs in a season. He won the MVP Award just once. What made him different was his ability to play so well for so long.

Aaron hit 44 home runs in 1957 when he was just 23 years old. He hit 40 home runs in 1973 at age 39. His nickname was "Hammering Hank" because of how hard he hit the ball. But he did not always swing for the fences. Aaron led the NL in doubles four times. He finished his career with 3,771 hits. That meant he had more than 3,000 hits that were not home runs.

Mickey Mantle once called Aaron "the best ball player" of his era—an era that Aaron defined with power, grace, and patience.

2,297

The number of RBIs Aaron collected during his career—a record that still stands.

The Braves' Hank Aaron hits his 710th career home run during a 1973 game against the San Francisco Giants.

HANK AARON

Positions: Outfielder and First Baseman

Hometown: Mobile, Alabama

Height, Weight: 6 feet, 180 pounds

Birth Date: February 5, 1934

Teams: Milwaukee/Atlanta Braves (1954–74)
Milwaukee Brewers (1975–76)

All-Star Games: 1955, 1956, 1957, 1958, 1959, 1960, 1961, 1962, 1963, 1964, 1965, 1966, 1967, 1968, 1969, 1970, 1971, 1972, 1973, 1974, 1975

Gold Gloves: 1958, 1959, 1960

MVP Award: 1957

FRANK ROBINSON

Frank Robinson's talent was easy to see. Strong. Fast. Brave. The outfielder spent 21 years in the major leagues. He beat opponents with his towering home runs and his fearless running on the base paths.

Robinson smashed 586 home runs in his career. He won the MVP Award in both the AL and the NL. And Robinson helped the Baltimore Orioles win two World Series titles.

Yet there was more to Robinson than how he played. He had a gift for working with other players. They respected him and would listen to him. That is why the Cleveland Indians made him a player/manager in 1975. Robinson would play in the game while also calling the shots. In doing so, he became the first black manager. Less than 30 years earlier, in 1947, Jackie Robinson had become the MLB's first black player.

Frank Robinson was a great power hitter and also a team leader.

"If I had one wish in the world today, it would be that Jackie Robinson could be here to see this happen," Robinson said when he got the job.

Yet Robinson's impact after his retirement was just as important. He helped pave the way for other minorities to become managers. And just as he had been a good player, Robinson was also a good manager.

The Baltimore Orioles had lost 107 games in 1988. Robinson then led them to an 87–75 record in 1989. It was one of the best turnarounds in baseball history. And for his efforts, Robinson was named AL Manager of the Year.

8

The number of home runs Robinson hit on Opening Day during his career—a record he shares with Ken Griffey Jr. and Adam Dunn.

The Baltimore Orioles' Frank Robinson hits a home run against the Detroit Tigers during a 1969 game.

FRANK ROBINSON

Positions: Outfielder and First Baseman

Hometown: Beaumont, Texas

Height, Weight: 6 feet 1, 183 pounds

Birth Date: August 31, 1935

Teams: Cincinnati Reds (1956–65)
Baltimore Orioles (1966–71)
Los Angeles Dodgers (1972)
California Angels (1973–74)
Cleveland Indians (1974–76)

All-Star Games: 1956, 1957, 1959, 1961, 1962,
1965, 1966, 1967, 1969, 1970, 1971, 1974

Gold Glove: 1958

MVP Awards: 1961, 1966

Rookie of the Year: 1956

PETE ROSE

The ball went rolling into center field.

So Pete Rose took off from second base. But he knew he had a chance to help the NL win the 1970 All-Star Game if he could score. So he quickly rounded third and headed for home.

The ball came in from the outfield. Rose set his sights on AL catcher Ray Fosse. Just as the ball reached home plate, Rose plowed into Fosse, sending him tumbling to the ground. Fans were not used to seeing such aggressive play at the All-Star Game. But Rose didn't earn the nickname "Charlie Hustle" for nothing.

Rose spent more than two decades playing baseball as if his life depended on it. There were other players who were more talented. However, few players could match Rose's intensity. His uniform always seemed to be dirty.

Pete Rose bulldozes through catcher Ray Fosse during a play at the plate in the 1970 All-Star Game.

Rose played mostly for the Cincinnati Reds and the Philadelphia Phillies during his 24 seasons. He wore down pitchers with his persistence. In 1985, he did the unthinkable when he broke Ty Cobb's record for career hits. He smashed the mark with a sharp single up the middle for his 4,192nd hit. He clapped his hands when he rounded first base. It was one of the few times he smiled while playing.

Rose finished his career with 4,256 hits. However, he is not in the Baseball Hall of Fame. In 1989, Rose was managing the Reds when he illegally bet on baseball games. Although he is one of the greatest players of all time, MLB banned him from the game.

15,890

The number of at-bats Rose had in his career—the most of any player in history.

Pete Rose of the Cincinnati Reds breaks Ty Cobb's career hits record with a line drive hit in 1985.

PETE ROSE

Positions: Outfielder and Infielder

Hometown: Cincinnati, Ohio

Birth Date: April 14, 1941

Height, Weight: 5 feet 11, 192 pounds

Teams: Cincinnati Reds (1963–78, 1984–86)
Philadelphia Phillies (1979–83)
Montreal Expos (1984)

All-Star Games: 1965, 1967, 1968, 1969, 1970,
1971, 1973, 1974, 1975, 1976, 1977, 1978,
1979, 1980, 1981, 1982, 1985

Gold Gloves: 1969, 1970

Silver Slugger: 1981

MVP Award: 1973

Rookie of the Year: 1963

ROD CAREW

Maybe it is only fitting that Rod Carew was born on a train. He was, after all, always on the move. Carew played 19 seasons with the Minnesota Twins and the California Angels. And he always seemed to be sprinting toward first after another big hit.

For Carew, hitting was a combination of art and science. He went by a set of rules that helped make him very consistent. His number one rule was "do not fear the baseball."

"You can't be afraid of being hit by the ball if you want to be a good hitter," he said.

Minnesota Twins infielder Rod Carew prepares for a pitch during a 1974 game.

Carew was not scared. But the pitchers who played against him certainly were. Three times in his career he led the majors in intentional walks. That meant that pitchers purposefully threw four straight balls to walk him rather than let Carew try to hit. Usually pitchers intentionally walk the most powerful sluggers. But only 92 of Carew's 3,053 career hits were home runs.

Part of that was by design. Carew never tried to swing for the fences. Instead, he would take whatever pitch came his way and carve it into the outfield for a single or a double. Carew led the AL in batting average seven times. He hit a career-high .388 in 1977 when he won the AL MVP Award.

Carew retired in 1985. But he still used his knowledge to help other hitters become great. He opened the Rod Carew Baseball School in 1987. It became a valuable resource for players and managers looking to learn more about the game.

33 million

The number of fan votes Carew received to the All-Star Game during his career. That helped him make the All-Star team 18 times.

Rod Carew of the California Angels acknowledges fans in 1985 after he recorded his 3,000th career hit.

ROD CAREW

Positions: First Baseman and Second Baseman

Hometown: Gatun, Canal Zone, Panama

Height, Weight: 6 feet, 170 pounds

Birth Date: October 1, 1945

Teams: Minnesota Twins (1967–78)
California Angels (1979–85)

All-Star Games: 1967, 1968, 1969, 1970, 1971, 1972, 1973, 1974, 1975, 1976, 1977, 1978, 1979, 1980, 1981, 1982, 1983, 1984

MVP Award: 1977

Rookie of the Year: 1967

BARRY BONDS

Some players can hit for average. Some can hit for power. Some can steal bases. Some can make great catches in the outfield. And then there was Barry Bonds, who could do everything.

Bonds combined Babe Ruth's power, Ty Cobb's hitting ability, and Roberto Clemente's arm. He could beat opponents in a handful of ways. But his method of choice was the home run.

The speedy outfielder won three NL MVP Awards early in his career. Two came while he was with the Pittsburgh Pirates. The third came after he moved to the San Francisco Giants in 1993. Then, starting in 2001, he won four more MVP Awards in a row as a record-smashing marvel.

San Francisco Giants left fielder Barry Bonds gets ready to hit his 740th career home run during a 2007 game.

Bonds set a single-season record for home runs when he smacked 73 for the Giants in 2001. Some of them would fly over the outfield wall at the Giants' ballpark and splash into the water behind the stadium. People would get into kayaks and wait for hours for the chance to grab one if Bonds went deep. And he went deep more than any player in history. He finished with 762 career home runs.

"Is he better than Babe Ruth? I don't know," former Atlanta Braves manager Bobby Cox said. "Barry never pitched and won 20 games. I know that. But in his era, there ain't nobody close. And I mean nobody."

However, critics suggested Bonds used illegal substances to get stronger later in his career. He denied the charges, pointing out that he never failed a drug test. Many believe the connection will still hurt his chances of making the Hall of Fame.

514

The number of bases Bonds stole in his career. Only 32 players in major league history had more through 2013.

Barry Bonds connects on his 739th career home run during a 2007 game against the Arizona Diamondbacks.

BARRY BONDS

Position: Left Fielder

Hometown: Riverside, California

Height, Weight: 6 feet 1, 185 pounds

Birth Date: July 24, 1964

Teams: Pittsburgh Pirates (1986–92)
San Francisco Giants (1993–2007)

All-Star Games: 1990, 1992–98, 2000–04, 2007

Gold Gloves: 1990–94, 1996–98

Silver Sluggers: 1990–94, 1996–97, 2000–04

MVP Awards: 1990, 1992, 1993, 2001, 2002, 2003, 2004

ALBERT PUJOLS

Ask Albert Pujols why he is such a great baseball player, and he will not talk about how strong he is or how hard he works. The key for Pujols is much simpler.

"I'm a really smart player," he said. "If you tell me something, I get it quickly. If there is something wrong with my hitting, tell me what's wrong and I'll pick it up right away."

Then again, there is rarely anything wrong with the way Pujols hits. He exploded onto the scene in 2001 with the St. Louis Cardinals. He hit 37 home runs in 2001 while winning Rookie of the Year. The guy they call "Prince Albert" was just getting started.

Los Angeles Angels first baseman Albert Pujols hits against the Kansas City Royals.

Pujols does not just swing from his heels and try to crush the ball. His goal is to get on base. And he does it better than anybody. He is the rare slugger who hardly ever strikes out. His teammates gave him the nickname "The Machine" because he is so steady it is almost like he is a robot.

Pujols's batting average for the first 10 years of his career never finished below .312. He also never hit fewer than 30 home runs through 2012. He had at least 99 RBIs in each of his first 12 seasons. It is no wonder he won three NL MVP Awards during that span.

Pujols has been just as dangerous in the playoffs. His career batting average in the postseason was .330 through 2013. He led the Cardinals to the World Series title in 2006 and 2011 before moving on to the Los Angeles Angels of Anaheim in 2012.

32

The number of first-place votes Pujols received for the 2001 NL Rookie of the Year Award. He is just one of 18 players to be the unanimous choice for the award through 2012.

The St. Louis Cardinals' Albert Pujols blasts a home run during the ninth inning of Game 3 of the 2011 World Series.

ALBERT PUJOLS

Positions: First Baseman and Outfielder

Hometown: Santo Domingo, Dominican Republic

Height, Weight: 6 feet 3, 230 pounds

Birth Date: January 16, 1980

Teams: St. Louis Cardinals (2001–11)
Los Angeles Angels of Anaheim (2012–)

All-Star Games: 2001, 2003, 2004, 2005, 2006, 2007, 2008, 2009, 2010

Gold Gloves: 2006, 2010

Silver Sluggers: 2001, 2003, 2004, 2008, 2009, 2010

MVP Awards: 2005, 2008, 2009

Rookie of the Year: 2001

HONORABLE MENTIONS

Johnny Bench – Arguably the best catcher ever, Bench won two MVP Awards and 10 Gold Gloves while powering the Cincinnati Reds to two World Series titles in the 1970s.

Roberto Clemente – The Pittsburgh Pirates' star outfielder ended his career in 1972 with exactly 3,000 hits. He died in the offseason on a humanitarian mission.

Ken Griffey Jr. – Known as "The Kid," Griffey hit 630 career home runs while playing mostly with the Seattle Mariners and the Cincinnati Reds in the 1990s and early 2000s.

Tony Gwynn – Gwynn, who played with the San Diego Padres in the 1980s and 1990s, ended his career with a .338 batting average. It was the highest by any player whose career began after 1950.

Reggie Jackson – Nicknamed "Mr. October" because of how well he played in the World Series, Jackson hit 563 home runs during his Hall of Fame career.

Eddie Murray – The switch-hitter racked up 504 home runs and collected 3,255 hits during his Hall of Fame career. He is considered the second-best switch-hitter ever after Mickey Mantle.

Cal Ripken Jr. – The Baltimore Orioles' star hit 345 home runs as a shortstop, the most ever by that position. He played a record 2,632 consecutive games between 1982 and 1998.

Mike Schmidt – Perhaps the best third baseman of all time, Schmidt hit 548 home runs and won the NL MVP Award three times with the Philadelphia Phillies.

Ichiro Suzuki – The Japanese superstar led major league baseball in hits seven times between 2001 and 2010.

Honus Wagner – The Pittsburgh Pirates hitter led the NL in batting average eight times and stolen bases five times before retiring in 1917.

GLOSSARY

base paths
The areas between bases used by runners to advance around the field.

doubleheader
A set of two baseball games played between the same two teams on the same day.

minorities
Groups of people who have less representation than other groups.

pennant
A long, triangular flag. In baseball, the word is used to describe a league championship.

postseason
The playoffs in which the top teams from the regular-season compete for a World Series title.

rookie
A first-year player in the major leagues.

switch-hitter
A batter who can hit from either side of the plate.

FOR MORE INFORMATION

Further Readings

National Baseball Hall of Fame and Museum. *Inside the Baseball Hall of Fame*. New York: Simon & Schuster, 2013.

Sports Illustrated Kids. *Sports Illustrated Kids Full Count: Top 10 Lists of Everything in Baseball*. New York: Time Home Entertainment Inc., 2012.

Web Links

To learn more about MLB's best hitters, visit ABDO Publishing Company online at **www.abdopublishing.com**. Web sites about MLB's best hitters are featured on our Book Links page. These links are routinely monitored and updated to provide the most current information available.

INDEX

ABOUT THE AUTHOR

Will Graves got hooked on baseball at age nine, when his father took him to his first Baltimore Orioles game. He has covered sports since 1996, and he joined the Associated Press in 2005. He currently works in Pittsburgh, Pennsylvania.